MW01172296

The Statue of Liberty
was a present from France

This wonderful gift they
were happy to finance

The idea came from
Edouard Rene de Laboulaye

Politician of the Anti-Slavery
movement of the day

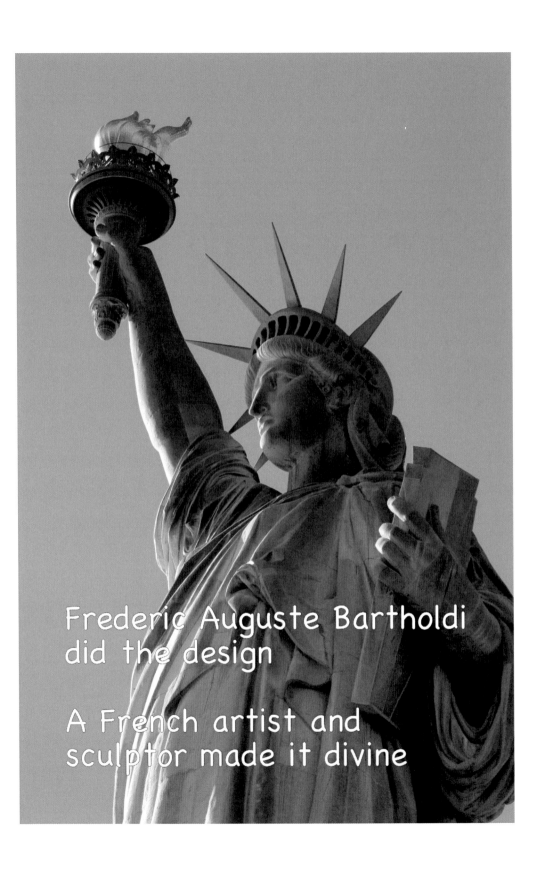

Frederic Auguste Bartholdi
did the design

A French artist and
sculptor made it divine

Frederic pitched the idea
to Americans for acceptance

To honor the centennial
of American Independence

The French raised
money to be created

To the United States
it would be donated

Frederic Bartholdi was
extremely prideful

Along with French
architect Gustave Eiffel

Sculptor's mother
modeled the face

Charlotte Bartholdi
did it with grace

Frederic produced
many sizes

Smaller ones were
his prizes

In his workshop
he sculpted

These grand
pieces resulted

Frederic completed the head
and torch-bearing arm

Exhibiting at international
expositions with charm

Introducing the Statue of Liberty was incredible

While waiting for the completion of the pedestal

It was constructed in France
and shipped in crates

This statue a magnificent
gift to the United States

Eiffel's iron framework was
the first piece reconstructed

Then hoisted up by steam
driven cranes as instructed

Molding light-weight copper
sheets to the Statue's skin

Hammering them onto the
wooden framework within

The copper statue to the torch is 46 meters in height

At 93 meters from the ground level is quite the sight

A big French flag was
draped over her face

For the unveiling
Frederic would showcase

The people of New York
City had a parade

A welcoming gesture
for what France made

Everyone cheered for
this important day

Freedom and justice is
what they would say

The statue was a
copper color to be seen

After time oxidation
turned it a patina green

Liberty Enlightening the World
was the original name

Subsequently Statue of
Liberty they would proclaim

On Liberty Island this
colossal neoclassical

This sculpture in New
York Harbor is magical

From France a gift of friendship recognized

A grand universal symbol of this great prize

People traveling to
America were excited

The gateway Ellis Island
they were invited

Packing their personal
belongings for the ship

Permanently in a travel
trunk for the big trip

Immigrants arriving at
Ellis Island with a gleam

The statue was a symbol
of the American dream

The Statue of Liberty for those traveling by sea

A symbol of democracy and a land for the free

Made in the USA
Columbia, SC
22 June 2023